STICKER ENCYCLOPEDIA

ANIMALS

REVISED EDITION

Senior Editor Jolyon Goddard
Project Editor Radhika Haswani
Assistant Editor Gunjan Mewati
Senior Designer Nidhi Mehra
Designers Charlotte Jennings, Seepiya Sahni
US Senior Editor Shannon Beatty
US Editor Margaret Parrish
Managing Editors Laura Gilbert,
Jonathan Melmoth, Alka Thakur Hazarika
Managing Art Editors Diane Peyton Jones,
Romi Chakraborty
DTP Designers Ashok Kumar, Sachin Gupta
Assistant Picture Researcher Nimesh Agrawal
Jacket Coordinator Issy Walsh
Jacket Designers Sonny Flynn, Rashika Kachroo
Jacket Editor Radhika Haswani
Pre-Production Producers David Almond, Sophie Chatellier
Senior Producer Ena Matagic
Delhi Team Head Malavika Talukder
Creative Director Helen Senior
Publishing Director Sarah Larter

Subject Consultant Kim Dennis-Bryan Ph.D., FZS

ORIGINAL EDITION

Author Andrea Pinnington
Senior Editor Sarah Davis
Designer Polly Appleton
Design Assistance Wendy Bartlet,
Fiona Gowen, Anne Sharples, Chloe Luxford
Jacket Designer Victoria Harvey
Acting Art Director Cathy Chesson
Publishing Manager Becky Hunter
Associate Publisher Sue Leonard
Production Controller Nick Seston
Senior Production Editor Vivianne Ridgeway
Production Editor Laragh Kedwell
Consultant Kim Dennis-Bryan Ph.D., FZS
Picture Researcher Kath Kollberg
US Editor Jennifer Quasha

MIX
Paper | Supporting
responsible forestry
FSC™ C018179

This book was made with Forest
Stewardship Council™ certified
paper—one small step in DK's
commitment to a sustainable future.
**For more information go to
www.dk.com/our-green-pledge**

About this book

HOW TO USE THIS BOOK

Read the information pages and then search for the relevant stickers in the back of the book to fill in the gaps. Use the sticker outlines and labels to help you.

There are lots of extra stickers that you can use to decorate the scenes in the back of the book. It's up to you where you put them all. The most important thing is to have lots of sticker fun!

DK would like to thank Kathleen Teece for editorial assistance and Cécile Landau for proofreading.

The publisher would like to thank the following for their kind permission
to reproduce their photographs:
(Key: a-above; b-below/bottom; c-center; f-far; l-left; r-right; t-top, row:column on pages 67, 70, 71)

3 Dorling Kindersley: Alan Murphy (crb). **Dreamstime.com**: Bigjohn3650 (bl). **5 Dreamstime.com**: Meunierd (br). **6–7 Dreamstime.com**: Nataliia Sokolovska (Background). **8–9 Dreamstime.com**: Wojphoto (Background). **9 Dreamstime.com**: Isselee (crb). **10–11 Dreamstime.com**: Grafner (Background). **11 Getty Images**: Purestock (tr). **12 Dreamstime.com**: Bradley Blackburn (bc).

12–13 Dreamstime.com: Natalya Erofeeva (Background). **14–15 Dreamstime.com**: Ulkass (Background). **16 naturepl.com**: Andrew Parkinson (clb). **16–17 Dreamstime.com**: Spectral-design. **18–19 Dreamstime.com**: Onassisworld (Background). **20–21 Dreamstime.com**: Sigitas Lukosevicius (Background). **22–23 Dreamstime.com**: Vladimir Melnikov (Background). **24–25 Dreamstime.com**: Hurry (Background). **26–27 Dreamstime.com**: Mofanto (Background). **27 iStockphoto.com**: Akinshin (clb). **28–29 Dreamstime.com**: Cmarkou (Background). **30–31 Dreamstime.com**: Grafner (Background). **32–33 Dreamstime.com**: Laszlo Mates (Background). **34–35 Dreamstime.com**: Maria Teresa Weinmann (Background). **36–37 iStockphoto.com**: Lingbeek. **38–39 Alamy Stock Photo**: ArteSub. **42 123RF.com**: Simon Eeman (bl). **Dreamstime.com**: Bigjohn3650 (tl); Kungverylucky (cra); Meunierd (cr); Isselee (cb, clb). **Getty Images**: Gerard Soury (c). **43 123RF.com**: Isselee (cl). **Ardea**: Doc White (bc). **Dorling Kindersley**: Harry Taylor (clb). **Dreamstime.com**: Jim Cumming (tc); Isselee (ca); Vladimir Melnik / Zanskar (bl). **46 Alamy Stock Photo**: David Wall (ca). **Avalon**: Daniel Heuclin (cb). **Dorling Kindersley**: Natural History Museum, London (cl). **Dreamstime.com**: Bradley Blackburn (fclb); Xavier Marchant / Xaviermarchant (tc); Oleksii Gotovyi (bl); Sergey Uryadnikov / Surz01 (fbl); Deaddogdodge (clb). **Getty Images**: Purestock (cla). **naturepl.com**: Andrew Parkinson (bc). **47 Dorling Kindersley**: Alan Murphy (ca); Exmoor Zoo, Devon (tc); The National Birds of Prey Centre, Gloucestershire (bl). **Dreamstime.com**: Agami Photo Agency (c); Mike Trewet (cra); Jan Pokorni / Pokec (fclb); Deaddogdodge (cb); Isselee (br); Vladimir Seliverstov / Vladsilver (clb). **50 Alamy Stock Photo**: Profimedia.CZ a.s. (cb/Turtle). **Dreamstime.com**: Amwu (cr); Isselee (cb). **iStockphoto.com**: Canoneer (tc). **naturepl.com**: Doug Perrine (c). **51 Alamy Stock Photo**: Scenics & Science (ftr). **Ardea**: Steve Downer (ca). **Dorling Kindersley**: Twan Leenders (clb). **Dreamstime.com**: Iulian Gherghel (tc); Isselee (tr). **54 123RF.com**: Isselee (cr). **Alamy Stock Photo**: Chris Luneski (cl); Wolfgang Pölzer (c). **Dorling Kindersley**: Natural History Museum, London (fcl); Exmoor Zoo, Devon (cb). **Dreamstime.com**: John Anderson (cra). **FLPA**: Fred Bavendam / Minden Pictures (br). **naturepl.com**: Ian Coleman (ca). **55 123RF.com**: Joseph Belanger (ca); Paulrommer (cl). **Alamy Stock Photo**: Martin Almqvist (tr); Jack Thomas (tc). **Ardea**: Pat Morris (crb). **Dreamstime.com**: Meisterphotos (br). **FLPA**: Fritz Polking (c). **58 123RF.com**: Isselee (cb/Panda). **Alamy Stock Photo**: Stefan Sollfors (tl). **Dreamstime.com**: Jim Cumming (clb); Isselee (cb, cb/Rhino). **FLPA**: Fred Bavendam / Minden Pictures (br). **59 Alamy Stock Photo**: Chris Luneski (bl). **Dorling Kindersley**: Natural History Museum, London (tl); Harry Taylor (cra). **Dreamstime.com**: Deaddogdodge (tl); Kungverylucky (cb); Xavier Marchant / Xaviermarchant (ca). **naturepl.com**: Ian Coleman (cla). **62 123RF.com**: Simon Eeman (c). **Ardea**: Doc White (cra). **Avalon**: Daniel Heuclin (cb, br). **Dorling Kindersley**: Harry Taylor (ca). **Dreamstime.com**: Eric Isselee (bl); Jan Pokorni / Pokec (tr). **Getty Images**: Gerard Soury (crb). **63 123RF.com**: Simon Eeman (cb/ Wild dog). **Alamy Stock Photo**: Stefan Sollfors (cr); Jack Thomas (ca); David Wall (br). **Dorling Kindersley**: Alan Murphy (ca). **Dreamstime.com**: Amwu (cb); John Anderson (tr); Kungverylucky (fcla); Bradley Blackburn (ca/Kangaroo); Xavier Marchant / Xaviermarchant (clb). **FLPA**: Fritz Polking (tl). **66 Alamy Stock Photo**: Jack Thomas (crb/fly). **Dorling Kindersley**: Alan Murphy (c); Natural History Museum, London (tc); Exmoor Zoo, Devon (cla). **Dreamstime.com**: John Anderson (tl); Meunier (ftl); Mike Trewet (tr); Bigjohn3650 (cra); Eric Isselee (fcra); Bradley Blackburn (ca); Vladimir Melnik / Zanskar (crb); Isselee (clb); Sergey Uryadnikov / Surz01 (cb); Oleksii Gotovyi (bcr); Vladimir Seliverstov / Vladsilver (bc). **Getty Images**: Purestock (ca/Blue Whale). **iStockphoto.com**: Canoneer (ca/Ostrich). **67 123RF.com**: Simon Eeman (1:7). **Alamy Stock Photo**: Scenics & Science (3:5); Jack Thomas (1:2, 3:7); David Wall (1:8, 3:1). **Ardea**: Steve Downer (3:3); Pat Morris (3:2). **Avalon**: Daniel Heuclin (2:6). **Dorling Kindersley**: Andrew Beckett (Illustration Ltd) (cra); Harry Taylor (2:2); Alan Murphy (cla/Yellow Warbler, 2:9). **Dreamstime.com**: John Anderson (1:1, ca); Bradley Blackburn (tr); Isselee (cla, fcl, cb, crb, c); Jan Pokorni / Pokec (clb); Kungverylucky (1:3); Vladimir Melnik / Zanskar (1:9). **Getty Images**: Purestock (3:6); Gerard Soury (1:4). **naturepl.com**: Andrew Parkinson (3:4). **70 123RF.com**: Simon Eeman (1:7); Paulrommer (5:3); Isselee (12:3). **Alamy Stock Photo**: Profimedia. CZ a.s. (4:2); David Wall (1:8, 5:4); Scenics & Science (3:5); Jack Thomas (3:7); Martin Almqvist (4:1); Chris Luneski (4:3); Wolfgang Pölzer (10:7); Stefan Sollfors (10:9). **Ardea**: Steve Downer (3:3); Pat Morris (3:2). **Avalon**: Daniel Heuclin (2:6). **Dorling Kindersley**: Alan Murphy (2:9); Harry Taylor (2:2); The National Birds of Prey Centre, Gloucestershire (9:5); Exmoor Zoo, Devon (7:2). **Dreamstime.com**: Agami Photo Agency (10:6); John Anderson (1:1); Kungverylucky (1:3); Vladimir Melnik / Zanskar (1:9); Bigjohn3650 (4:4); Amwu (4:6); Isselee (4:7, 5:5, 10:5, 12:6, 13:6, 12:7); Deaddogdodge (4:8); Meisterphotos (7:7); Meunierd (11:5); Jim Cumming (12:1); Sergey Uryadnikov / Surz01 (13:9); Jan Pokorni / Pokec (13:7); Oleksii Gotovyi (13:2); Bradley Blackburn (7:4, 5:1). **FLPA**: Fred Bavendam / Minden Pictures (4:5, 7:1). **Getty Images**: Purestock (3:6); Gerard Soury (1:4, 8:4). **iStockphoto.com**: Canoneer (5:9). **naturepl.com**: Andrew Parkinson (3:4); Doug Perrine (6:7). **71 123RF.com**: Simon Eeman (7:7, 13:7); Paulrommer (12:3). **Alamy Stock Photo**: Profimedia.CZ a.s. (11:2); David Wall (7:8, 13:8, 5:4); Scenics & Science (2:9); Martin Almqvist (11:1); Chris Luneski (11:3); Wolfgang Pölzer (5:7); Stefan Sollfors (5:9); Jack Thomas (4:7). **Ardea**: Pat Morris (3:3). **Avalon**: Daniel Heuclin (8:6). **Dorling Kindersley**: Andrew Beckett (Illustration Ltd) (4:1); Harry Taylor (7:2); Exmoor Zoo, Devon (10:2); Alan Murphy (3:6, 8:9, 2:2). **Dreamstime.com**: Agami Photo Agency (5:6); John Anderson (13:1); Kungverylucky (7:3, 12:2, 13:3); Vladimir Melnik / Zanskar (7:9, 13:9); Bigjohn3650 (1:6, 11:4); Amwu (6:8, 11:6); Deaddogdodge (11:8); Meisterphotos (10:7); Isselee (2:3, 5:5, 12:5, 1:2, 11:7); Sergey Uryadnikov / Surz01 (8:2); Vladimir Seliverstov / Vladsilver (1:1); Bradley Blackburn (10:4, 12:1, 1:3). **FLPA**: Fred Bavendam / Minden Pictures (10:1, 11:5). **Getty Images**: Gerard Soury (7:4, 13:4). **iStockphoto.com**: Canoneer (12:9). **naturepl.com**: Doug Perrine (2:8, 9:7).

Cover images: *Front*: **Dreamstime.com**: Eric Isselee c, Isselee clb, Subbotina (Background), Mike Trewet cla; *Back*: **123RF.com**: Isselee tr; **Dorling Kindersley**: Exmoor Zoo, Devon cla; **Dreamstime.com**: John Anderson tc, Meunierd crb, Subbotina (Background)

All other images © Dorling Kindersley

Contents

Mammals	4	Lizards	21
Primates	5	Snakes	22
Cats	6	Crocodiles and alligators	23
Dogs	7	Amphibians	24
Bears	8	Frogs and toads	25
Land giants	9	Salamanders and newts	26
Marine mammals	10	Fish	27
Ocean giants	11	Sharks and rays	28
Marsupials	12	Bony fish	29
Birds	13	Invertebrates	30
Songbirds	14	Mollusks	31
Freshwater birds	15	Strange sea creatures	32
Sea birds	16	Crustaceans	33
Birds of prey	17	Insects	34
Flightless birds	18	Spiders and scorpions	35
Reptiles	19		
Tortoises and turtles	20	Sticker fun!	36–71

Mammals

You are a mammal! Like most mammals, you have the following characteristics: you can control your body temperature; you have a backbone; you have hair on your body; and, if you are female, you feed your young with the milk you produce.

RECORD-BREAKING MAMMALS

 Slowest: Sloth

 Largest: Blue whale

 Smallest: Kitti's hog-nosed bat

 Largest brain: Sperm whale

 Highest living: Large-eared pika

Dromedary
Camelus dromedarius
This one-humped camel is able to live in very hot places such as deserts. It has two rows of eyelashes to keep sand out of its face, and it doesn't need to drink much water.

Brown long-eared bat
Plecotus auritus
This bat is good at finding insects in the dark. It makes clicking noises and waits for the echoes to bounce off the insects.

Large hairy armadillo
Chaetophractus villosus
This armadillo uses its sharp claws for digging burrows and finding food. It lives in dry places in South America.

Primates

Many primates live in trees in tropical rain forests. The size of their brains is large compared to their bodies, which explains why they are such intelligent animals. They usually live in large groups.

Black-capped squirrel monkey
Saimiri boliviensis

Squirrel monkeys live in huge groups called troops. This one is found in the rain forests of Bolivia and Peru. Its tail is longer than its head and body.

Ring-tailed lemur
Lemur catta

Lemurs come from the island of Madagascar, in the Indian Ocean. Ring-tailed lemurs live in groups of up to 30 family members.

South African galago
Galago moholi

This is also known as a bush baby. It sleeps during the day, huddled next to other galagos. At night, it hunts for insects.

Western gorilla
Gorilla gorilla

The largest of all primates, the western gorilla lives in forests, feeding on fruits, seeds, and plants. The male has a silver back and is twice the size of the female. Gorillas move around by walking on their knuckles.

FACT!

Gorillas can make up to 17 noises, such as grunts, laughs, and screams. They each have a specific meaning.

Cats

Cats are covered in soft fur that is often striped or spotted. They are expert hunters with keen senses, flexible bodies, and sharp teeth and claws. Small cats mostly hunt for rodents and birds.

Bobcat
Lynx rufus

Unlike most cats, the bobcat has a short tail. It lives in North America in forests, grasslands, and deserts. The bobcat mostly feeds on rabbits and hares.

Domestic cat
Felis catus

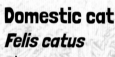

These cats are found in most parts of the world. They are mainly kept as pets and have little need for hunting. More than 100 breeds of domestic cat exist today.

Tiger
Panthera tigris

This is the largest member of the cat family. Six types of tiger exist today, and three others have become extinct. Even though they are in danger of dying out, tigers are still hunted and their habitats are at risk.

Lion
Panthera leo

Lions are the only cats to live in groups, called prides. Pride sizes vary from 4 to 37 members, but the average size is 15. The adult lions in the group look after all the cubs together.

DID YOU KNOW?
Lions, tigers, leopards, and jaguars are the only cats that can roar. The others purr, chirp, or even bark!

Dogs

Domestic dogs are kept as pets, but all other dogs are wild. Dogs are effective hunters with their sharp teeth and good sense of smell. Most have short fur and long, bushy tails.

Gray wolf
Canis lupus

This is the heaviest wild member of the dog family. Gray wolves live in packs, and they howl to warn neighboring packs off their territory. All pet dogs are descendants of the gray wolf.

African wild dog
Lycaon pictus

These dogs are also known as "painted dogs" because of their beautiful markings. They live in large packs of 30 or more and work together to hunt and take care of their puppies.

FACT!

Wolves use facial expressions, body language, sound, and smell to communicate with each other.

Red fox
Vulpes vulpes

The red fox tends to hunt at night. It has become a common sight in towns and cities, where it raids trash cans for food.

Maned wolf
Chrysocyon brachyurus

This long-legged wolf from South America is sometimes described as a "red fox on stilts." It feeds on small animals, such as rabbits and mice.

Bears

Bears are large mammals with heavy bodies, thick legs, and short tails. They live mainly in forests and eat plants as well as meat. Their large, strong paws can kill with a single blow.

Polar bear
Ursus maritimus
Polar bears live in the icy north, feeding mostly on seals. Their dense fur and thick body fat help keep them warm in the cold. Male polar bears weigh almost twice as much as females.

Giant panda
Ailuropoda melanoleuca
This bear feeds for about 13 hours a day on bamboo shoots. Its cubs are only 6 in (15 cm) long at birth and have little fur. Pandas are in danger of dying out as bamboo forests are being chopped down.

Brown bear
Ursus arctos
The brown bear lives for about 25 years. It eats roots, bulbs, plants, and meat from spring to fall, and then sleeps during the winter months.

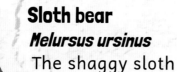

Sloth bear
Melursus ursinus
The shaggy sloth bear eats ants and termites that it sucks up through a gap in its teeth. The female usually has one or two cubs at a time.

DID YOU KNOW?
Not all big animals have big babies: a newborn polar bear cub is about the size of a guinea pig.

Land giants

Here are some of the largest and most incredible animals that live on land. Despite their size, they are peaceful animals unless threatened or provoked.

Hippopotamus
Hippopotamus amphibius

Even though the hippopotamus has a large body, it can trot very quickly on land and walk gracefully in water. It eats about 90 lb (41 kg) of grass each day.

White rhinoceros
Ceratotherium simum

This is the second-largest land animal after the elephant. The hump on its shoulders is made up of muscle and is needed to support its huge head! Despite its large head, the rhino's brain is, in fact, very small.

Giraffe
Giraffa camelopardalis

The giraffe is the tallest living animal. It uses its long neck to reach up and eat leaves from trees.

Asian elephant
Elephas maximus

Elephants are the giants of all land animals. The biggest one ever found weighed as much as 150 people! Some, like this one, have no tusks.

Marine mammals

There are 130 types of marine mammals. Some live only in water, and others live on land and in water. Unlike fish, they use vertical rather than sideways body movements.

Common bottlenose dolphin
Tursiops truncatus
This is the dolphin you are most likely to see if you go to an aquarium or a theme park. It is known for being curious and friendly toward humans.

West Indian manatee
Trichechus manatus
This large, slow-moving creature feeds only on plants. Its continual grazing wears out its teeth, but old molars are constantly replaced by new ones at the back of its jaws.

Walrus
Odobenus rosmarus
Walruses mostly eat mollusks, diving to the bottom of the ocean to find them. The longest recorded walrus dive lasted 24 minutes. Male walruses use their long tusks to fight other males.

FACT!
If a dolphin is ill or hurt, members of its family will often help it.

New Zealand sea lion
Phocarctos hookeri
Sea lions live both on land and in water. This sea lion only lives on a few islands off New Zealand, and it eats crabs, fish, and penguins.

Ocean giants

Here are some more mammals that live in the sea. Like land mammals, they breathe air, give birth to live young, and then suckle them with their milk.

Narwhal
Monodon monoceros
Narwhals live in the Arctic Ocean in huge groups, called schools. Males have a long tooth that grows through their lip. They use this to spar with other male narwhals.

Orca
Orcinus orca
The orca, or killer whale, is the largest member of the dolphin family. It lives in family groups, called pods. Pods often join together to form superpods of up to 150 orcas!

Blue whale
Balaenoptera musculus
This is the world's largest mammal. It can be 112 ft (34 m) long and weigh up to 190 tons (172 metric tons). Despite its huge size, it eats tiny shrimplike creatures, called krill.

Sperm whale
Physeter macrocephalus
The box-shaped head of the sperm whale is up to one-third of its total body length. It can dive to great depths and remain underwater for up to an hour.

Marsupials

Most marsupials have pouches to carry their young. Tiny newborns spend a lot of their time growing in this pouch, rather than in their mother's belly. Most live in Australasia.

Red kangaroo
Macropus rufus
This is the largest of all marsupials. It lives in Australia in grassy areas. It uses its long legs for jumping and its tail for balance.

Virginia opossum
Didelphis virginiana
When in danger, this American marsupial pretends to be dead. It lies still for up to six hours, with its eyes and mouth open.

Common wombat
Vombatus ursinus
This furry, bearlike marsupial lives in a burrow. It usually has one baby at a time, which stays in its mother's pouch for about 10 months.

Tasmanian devil
Sarcophilus harrisii
This ratlike animal lives on the island of Tasmania, south of Australia. It lives in burrows and hunts at night, gathering in groups at the site of a kill.

DID YOU KNOW?
Baby kangaroos, or joeys, are tiny when born—about 1 in (2.5 cm) long.

Birds

Birds form one of the most colorful animal groups. Many are known for their tuneful ways of communicating with each other. All of them have backbones, lay eggs, and are warm-blooded. Birds are the only animals to have feathers, and most use their wings to fly.

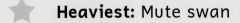
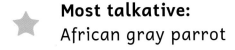
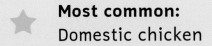
Arctic tern
Sterna paradisaea
The Arctic tern flies about 44,000 miles (70,800 km) a year! This is the longest distance of any bird. It travels from the far north down to Antarctica in the south.

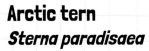

Barn owl
Tyto alba
The barn owl has incredible vision and hearing, which make it a fearsome hunter. It flies low over the ground, listening for the sound of animals, and then swoops!

Toco toucan
Ramphastos toco
The toucan's bill looks heavy, but it is, in fact, very light. This bird lives in holes in trees and makes a deep snoring sound.

Songbirds

More than half of the world's bird species make up a huge family known as songbirds, or perching birds. Most of them sing, but some have harsh calls. These birds are usually small, and their feet can grip well.

Yellow warbler
Setophaga petechia

There are many different types of warbler, and they are known for their different songs, including a scolding song.

Blue tit
Cyanistes caeruleus

This small, stocky songbird makes lots of different sounds, from trilling songs to high-pitched whistles. It sings all year but is most often heard between February and June.

DID YOU KNOW?

Songbirds' feet have three toes pointing forward and one toe pointing backward. This helps them grip onto thin branches.

Bullock's oriole
Icterus bullockii

This oriole lives in woodlands in the western United States but flies south to Central America in the winter. The male and female have different songs. The female's is harsher, but she sings more often!

European starling
Sturnus vulgaris

Also called the common starling, this noisy bird is very good at mimicking sounds, especially whistles!

14

Freshwater birds

Freshwater rivers, lakes, and wetland areas are home to a huge number of colorful and interesting birds. Most of them feed on water plants, insects, fish, and other small animals.

Black-crowned night heron
Nycticorax nycticorax

As its name suggests, this heron hunts at night. It eats food such as frogs, insects, and fish. Its long flexible toes help it to balance, so it doesn't sink in soft mud.

Lesser flamingo
Phoeniconaias minor

This is the smallest type of flamingo. It lives in massive flocks of up to a million birds on the salty lakes of Africa.

FACT!

Flamingos are pink because they eat large amounts of shrimp, which color their feathers pink.

Mallard
Anas platyrhynchos

The mallard is known as a dabbling duck. This is because it feeds at the surface of the water and doesn't dive for food. Only the male duck is colorful like this one.

Black swan
Cygnus atratus

This bird is only found in Australia in large lakes, lagoons, and bays. It forms huge flocks with tens of thousands of birds.

Sea birds

During the breeding season, most sea birds form colonies (large groups) by the sea. They usually have fewer chicks than other birds but spend a lot of time caring for them.

Wandering albatross
Diomedea exulans
Albatrosses have the largest wingspan of all birds. This allows them to soar for hours in the air without flapping their wings. They build their nests on land and lay one egg every other year.

Brown pelican
Pelecanus occidentalis
The pelican uses its big bill to catch fish for itself and its young. It spots fish from the air and dives to catch them.

Great cormorant
Phalacrocorax carbo
Cormorants live in most watery areas, not just the sea. They can swim swiftly underwater and their hooked bills are good for catching fish.

Atlantic puffin
Fratercula arctica
Unlike most birds, the colorful puffin nests in burrows, under boulders, or in cracks between rocks. The female lays one egg, and both parents care for the new chick.

FACT!
A bird's wingspan is the distance from one outstretched wing tip to the other.

Birds of prey

Eagles, hawks, and vultures are all birds of prey. These birds have huge wings, sharp claws, hooked beaks, and amazing eyesight. They hunt during the day and eat many types of animals.

Red–tailed hawk
Buteo jamaicensis
This bird has a hoarse scream that it makes when soaring. Its diet varies, depending on where it lives, but it preys on small mammals, snakes, frogs, and other birds.

Common kestrel
Falco tinnunculus
This bird spots prey by sight, hovers over it, and then swoops down to grab it. It eats birds and small mammals, such as voles.

Bald eagle
Haliaeetus leucocephalus
The bald eagle is the national bird of the United States. It usually nests in trees, but it will nest on the ground or on cliffs in coastal areas.

Secretary bird
Sagittarius serpentarius
This bird hunts animals such as snakes, frogs, and insects. It runs after its prey and then stamps on it to kill it.

DID YOU KNOW?
The eagle is the most powerful bird of prey. It can kill mammals as big as itself.

Flightless birds

Even though all birds have wings, not all of them can fly. Some flightless birds run well, while others are great swimmers.

Common ostrich
Struthio camelus

This is the world's tallest and heaviest bird. It can't fly, but it can run really fast. The male has black feathers on its back and the female's are gray-brown.

King penguin
Aptenodytes patagonicus

Penguins are great swimmers and divers. They use their wings as flippers when underwater. During the breeding season, king penguins live in huge colonies. Both parents take turns looking after the chick.

FACT!

The ostrich is the only bird in the world to have just two toes on each foot.

Brown kiwi
Apteryx mantelli

The kiwi is New Zealand's national bird. It lives in forests and looks for food at night. Its shrill whistle can be heard after sunset.

Southern cassowary
Casuarius casuarius

This strange-looking bird is very shy but will fight fiercely if attacked. The growth on its head, called a casque, may be used to help control body temperature.

Reptiles

Reptiles live on land and in water. They have backbones and tough, waterproof skin. They are cold-blooded, so their body temperature depends on their surroundings. Reptiles bask in the sun to warm up and seek shade to cool down. Most lay eggs, rather than giving birth to live young.

Green tree python
Morelia viridis
The green tree python blends perfectly into the trees it lives in. It catches food by wrapping itself around a branch and then striking out at passing prey.

Tuatara
Sphenodon punctatus
These reptiles grow very slowly and can live to be more than 100 years old. At rest, they may only breathe once an hour! They feed mainly on crickets and beetles.

African helmeted turtle

Pelomedusa subrufa
In the rainy season, this turtle wanders between rain pools looking for food such as frogs and invertebrates. If threatened, it withdraws into its shell.

Tortoises and turtles

These animals have lived on Earth since the time of the dinosaurs. Tortoises live on land and turtles live in water. Their hard shells protect their bodies and help them hide from enemies.

Galápagos tortoise
Chelonoidis nigra
This is the largest tortoise in the world and grows up to 6 ft (1.8 m) long. It grazes in herds in the Galápagos Islands off South America. Some live to be 100 years old!

Leatherback turtle
Dermochelys coriacea
This turtle has a leathery shell and clawless flippers. It dives for jellyfish, holding its breath for up to half an hour. The female lays eggs on sandy beaches at night.

Red-eared slider
Trachemys scripta elegans
This turtle has a bold red stripe behind its eyes. It lives in lakes and rivers in North America, where it loves to bask in the sunshine.

FACT!
A turtle's shell contains about 60 bones connected together with a covering of tough plates made of keratin.

Indian starred tortoise
Geochelone elegans
The shell of this tortoise is very bumpy, making it very hard to bite! The Indian starred tortoise needs a lot of water and is only really active during the rainy season.

Lizards

Lizards are scaly and generally have four legs, although some have no legs at all. If attacked, their tails break off, giving them a chance to escape, while the predator eats the tail.

Slow worm
Anguis fragilis

The slow worm looks more like a snake than a lizard, since it has no legs. It is one of the few reptiles that give birth to live young rather than laying eggs.

Gila monster
Heloderma suspectum

The bright colors of this North American lizard warn other animals that it is venomous—it injects a poison when it bites.

DID YOU KNOW?

The fastest lizard is the black iguana. It can run at almost 22 mph (35 kph).

Panther chameleon
Furcifer pardalis

Chameleons can change color to match their surroundings! They catch insects by flicking out their incredibly long elastic tongue.

Plumed basilisk
Basiliscus plumifrons

Also known as the Jesus Christ lizard, this lizard can run for short distances across the water's surface (on its hind legs) to escape its enemies.

Snakes

Snakes are reptiles with no legs. They move along the ground or in the water by wriggling their bodies. Some snakes are venomous, although only a few can kill humans.

Common garter snake
Thamnophis sirtalis
This North American snake lives near water and during winter it goes into a sleeplike state called hibernation. Females give birth to live young rather than laying eggs.

Yellow anaconda
Eunectes notaeus
This snake can reach 13 ft (4 m) in length. It wraps itself around its prey, such as birds and caimans, and squeezes them to death.

Red spitting cobra
Naja pallida
A cobra is dangerous from the moment it hatches. This African one squirts venom out of its fangs at its enemies. The poison doesn't kill, but it can cause blindness.

Adder (Common viper)
Vipera berus
All adders have zigzag markings on their backs, although their bodies may vary in color. They like to lie in the sunshine, but during winter they hibernate.

DID YOU KNOW?
Baby snakes have a special tooth for breaking out of their eggshells.

Crocodiles and alligators

Crocodiles and alligators are large reptiles that have changed little since the age of the dinosaurs. They have long snouts, flat bodies, short legs, and powerful tails. They all eat meat!

Spectacled caiman
Caiman crocodilus

Hunted for its skin, the caiman is almost always in water. It floats by day and becomes active at night, when it looks for amphibians, reptiles, and waterbirds to eat.

Gharial
Gavialis gangeticus

The male gharial has a bulb on the end of its long, thin snout that makes the sound it produces underwater louder. It can't walk far on land because its legs are too short and weak.

FACT!

The saltwater crocodile is the largest reptile alive today. Males grow up to 23 ft (7 m) long.

Nile crocodile
Crocodylus niloticus

Like all crocodiles, this one can bite but it can't chew. It catches and drowns large animals. Then it twists and turns them underwater to tear off pieces of meat.

American alligator
Alligator mississippiensis

This alligator lives in lakes and swamps. The female lays up to 60 eggs in a huge nest and may stay with her young for three years.

Amphibians

These cold-blooded animals are divided into three main groups: newts and salamanders; frogs and toads; and caecilians. Most undergo some sort of transformation from birth to adulthood. For example, most frogs start off as eggs, turn into tadpoles, and then grow into adult frogs.

DID YOU KNOW?
A group of frogs is called a chorus.

Golden mantella
Mantella aurantiaca
This small frog is only about 1 in (2.5 cm) long. It is poisonous, and its bright color warns enemies to keep away.

Purple caecilian
Gymnopis multiplicata
Caecilians have no limbs and look like worms or snakes. They are hardly ever seen because they live either underground or in water.

Fire salamander
Salamandra salamandra
This salamander lives in woody areas and eats insects, spiders, earthworms, and slugs. Each one has different markings.

Frogs and toads

Unlike lizards, adult frogs and toads have long back legs and no tail. Most frogs hop, live in or near water, and have smooth skin. Most toads walk, live on land, and have rough, warty bodies.

Red-eyed tree frog
Agalychnis callidryas
This frog's green color keeps it well hidden in trees, which it climbs with the help of sticky pads on its feet. Its bright red eyes help it see at night.

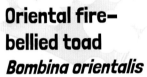

Oriental fire-bellied toad
Bombina orientalis
The green back of this oriental fire-bellied toad hides it well in the forest. If attacked, it flashes its red belly, warning other animals that it is poisonous.

Cuyaba dwarf frog
Physalaemus nattereri

When threatened, this frog puffs up its body and stands up, extending its back legs. This, in turn, lifts the false eyes and makes the frog look like a larger animal.

Southern leopard frog
Rana sphenocephala
Most frogs and toads can sit very still for a long time, waiting for insects to pass by. When disturbed, this one makes for the nearest water in a series of zigzag leaps.

FACT!
Frogs and toads croak or call. Each has a unique call that may be made louder by vocal sacs in the neck.

Salamanders and newts

Salamanders and newts have thin bodies and long tails. They are found living both in water and on land. Most adult salamanders have lungs, but some, such as the aquatic species, have external gills.

Tiger salamander
Ambystoma tigrinum
The female salamander lays up to 7,000 eggs in one season! They hatch in water but usually live on land when they are adults.

Axolotl
Ambystoma mexicanum
These animals are unusual because they can breed even though they usually remain in their larval (young) form with gills. They can only survive in water.

Great crested newt
Triturus cristatus
Also called the warty newt, the male attracts females by doing a strange underwater dance! Females lay one egg at a time and wrap it in leaves for protection.

Mandarin salamander
Tylototriton verrucosus
Otherwise known as the crocodile or emperor newt, this small amphibian lives in the cool forests of Asia. Its orange warts produce foul substances if it is attacked.

Fish

The first fish lived on Earth more than 500 million years ago! Fish have evolved into creatures of enormous variety, both in shape and color. They are cold-blooded and most have gills for breathing, scales covering them, and fins for movement.

RECORD-BREAKING FISH

 Largest: Whale shark

 Smallest: *Paedocypris progenetica*

 Fastest: Black marlin

 Most venomous: Stonefish

 Most eggs laid: Ocean sunfish

DID YOU KNOW?

There are more than 33,000 living species of fish in the world.

Emperor angelfish
Pomacanthus imperator

If a male angelfish dies, one of the females in its family group will change sex and become the dominant fish!

Longnose gar
Lepisosteus osseus

Lurking among underwater plants, this long fish waits for prey to come near it and then darts forward to attack!

Common clown fish
Amphiprion ocellaris

This colorful fish lives among sea anemones. It is protected from the stinging tentacles of the sea anemone by a special substance covering its body.

Sharks and rays

Sharks and rays have skeletons that are made of cartilage rather than bone. Many shark species are in danger of dying out because of overfishing for their fins to make shark-fin soup. Both sharks and rays can be dangerous to humans.

Round stingray
Urobatis halleri
This ray has a painful sting that can cause minor injuries. Compared to other stingrays, its body is much rounder and its tail is shorter.

Great white shark
Carcharodon carcharias
Although this shark has a reputation for being a man-eater, it rarely attacks people. It mainly feeds on seals, dolphins, and big fish.

Blacktip reef shark
Carcharhinus melanopterus
This shark is a powerful swimmer. The black tips of its fins are often seen in shallow, warm tropical waters.

Smooth hammerhead
Sphyrna zygaena
Hammerhead sharks have very strange-shaped heads. Their eyes lie at the end of each head flap. They feed on fish and even other small sharks, and in summer they form schools to migrate to cooler waters.

Bony fish

Most fish are bony fish. Their tail fin propels them forward, while the other fins provide control and stability. Most have an air sac called a "swim bladder" for buoyancy. They are found in the ocean as well as rivers and lakes.

Sockeye salmon
Oncorhynchus nerka

This salmon hatches in a river and then makes its way to the sea to mature. As an adult, it returns to the same river to breed. Its color changes as it moves from salt to fresh water.

Goldfish
Carassius auratus

Goldfish are the most common fish to be kept as pets. They usually live for about six years, although the oldest recorded one lived to be 49 years old!

Red piranha
Pygocentrus nattereri

This harmless-looking fish has sharp teeth and powerful jaws. It usually scavenges for food, but it will hunt in packs in shallow water. It has a silver back and a red underside.

FACT!

There are about 31,000 different species of bony fish alive today.

Lionfish
Pterois sp.

Lionfish are generally striped and have long, venomous spines that are deadly to their prey. Their stripes warn other fish to keep away.

Invertebrates

Invertebrates were the first animals on Earth. Today, they make up most of the animals in the world in every kind of habitat. They include insects, spiders, crabs, sponges, worms, shellfish, and many more. Invertebrates do not have a backbone.

RECORD-BREAKING INVERTEBRATES

 Longest animal:
Bootlace worm

 Longest-lived insect:
Termite queen

 Heaviest insect:
Goliath beetle

 Most venomous spider:
Brazilian wandering spider

Common European earthworm
Lumbricus terrestris
These familiar creatures spend most of their time underground. They are eaten by birds and moles.

Bumblebee
Bombus sp.
Bees travel from flower to flower, busily pollinating plants. They carry the pollen in baskets on their back legs.

Giant Pacific octopus
Enteroctopus dofleini
This is the largest octopus in the world. With its arms outstretched, it can be as big as three people lined up head to toe.

DID YOU KNOW?
Octopuses can squeeze through tiny holes—the only hard part of their body is their beak.

Mollusks

Mollusks are a very varied group. Some have heads with well-developed eyes, such as squid and octopuses. Others have shells and a muscular foot. Snails make up the largest group. The mollusks on this page live in the sea.

European squid
Loligo vulgaris
Squid swim slowly by rippling their fins. To move faster, they expel jets of water from their bodies. Many types can release a cloud of ink to help them escape from predators.

Common limpet
Patella vulgata
This limpet clings to rocks and wanders around looking for algae to feed on. It has a cone-shaped shell to protect it.

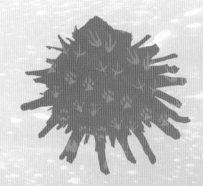

Atlantic thorny oyster
Spondylus americanus
This oyster's shell can be white with orange or purple areas. The shell differs from other oysters because it has sharp spikes on it.

Lined chiton
Tonicella lineata
The lined chiton has a large foot that it uses to crawl over the seabed looking for food. It also uses it to grip onto rocks. Its shell is made up of eight sections.

FACT!

The American oyster produces up to 64 million eggs a year—but usually only one reaches adulthood!

Strange sea creatures

The sea contains some of the most amazing animals in the world. One of the animals on this page has a deadly sting—read on to see which one.

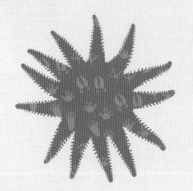

Common sun star
Crossaster papposus
Most starfish have five arms, but the common sun star has between eight and sixteen. It moves slowly using hundreds of tubelike feet.

Purple sea urchin
Strongylocentrotus purpuratus
Sea urchins don't have brains! Their sharp spines are for protection and work with their soft "tube feet" to help them move.

Box jellyfish
Chironex fleckeri
This is one of the most dangerous animals in the world. Its stinging tentacles carry enough venom to kill more than 60 people! It is found in the waters around northern Australia.

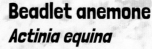

Beadlet anemone
Actinia equina
The anemone extends its tentacles underwater. When it is above water, such as at low tide, it withdraws its tentacles and looks like a blob of jelly.

Crustaceans

Most crustaceans live in water, although some have adapted to life on land. They all have skeletons on the outside of their bodies, called exoskeletons, which they have to molt, or shed, in order to grow.

Gooseneck barnacles
Pollicipes polymerus
This barnacle has a stalk. It lives on rocky shores in the northeastern Pacific Ocean. It sometimes attaches itself to boats and other floating objects too.

Pill woodlouse
Armadillidium vulgare
This woodlouse, unlike some other types, can roll up into a ball if attacked. It lives in damp, dark places and comes out at night to feed on rotting plants.

DID YOU KNOW?
Crabs have sensory hairs on their antennas, which they use to detect smells in the water.

Fiddler crab
Uca vocans
Only the male fiddler crab has the large claw you can see above. When it molts, the crab hides until its new shell has hardened.

Caribbean spiny lobster
Panulirus argus
Man is the lobster's biggest enemy! They are also eaten by octopuses, sharks, and skates. Spiny lobsters do not have big pincerlike claws.

Insects

All insects have six legs and many have wings. They live throughout the world and there are more than a million different types. Here are just a few.

Monarch butterfly
Danaus plexippus
The monarch travels hundreds of miles in its short life. Huge numbers of them spend winter sleeping in woodlands in California and Mexico.

Housefly
Musca domestica
Female houseflies lay five to six batches of up to 100 eggs over several days. Maggots hatch from the eggs and transform into flies in as little as a week.

Golden scarab
Chrysina resplendens
The scarab beetle was a holy animal in ancient Egypt and its image is found on many of the pharaohs' tombs. The metallic-colored scarab, here, lives in Central America.

Southern hawker
Aeshna cyanea
Also called the blue hawker, this is one of the largest of all dragonflies. It has two sets of wings and very large eyes, and it is found by ponds and rivers.

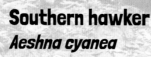

Spiders and scorpions

Insects have six legs, but spiders and scorpions have eight. All spiders produce silk, which may be used for spinning webs, catching insects, moving around, and making egg cases.

Jumping spider
Marpissa muscosa
There are more than 6,000 species of jumping spider. They have eight eyes and pounce on their prey. This type is furry with a flat body.

Mexican red-kneed tarantula
Brachypelma hamorii
This hairy spider's body grows to just over 2 in (5 cm). It lives on its own and spends most of its time in its burrow.

Imperial scorpion
Pandinus imperator
This scorpion can reach 8 in (20 cm) in length. Despite their fierce appearance, females care for their young for the first few weeks of life, carrying them around on their backs.

Black widow
Latrodectus mactans
This spider has a poisonous bite, but the female is more venomous than the male. After mating, the female sometimes kills and eats the male.

Grassland

CHECKLIST

Use the stickers in the book to fill up the scene. Here are some animals that live in grasslands. Which is your favorite?

- [ ] White rhinoceros
- [ ] Giraffe
- [ ] Maned wolf
- [ ] Red spitting cobra
- [ ] Secretary bird
- [ ] Tiger
- [ ] Red-tailed hawk

Ocean

CHECKLIST

Use the stickers in this book to fill the ocean scene. Here are some animals that live in coastal areas. Can you find any others?

- [ ] West Indian manatee
- [ ] Common sun star
- [ ] Lionfish
- [ ] Orca
- [ ] Arctic tern
- [ ] European squid
- [ ] Box jellyfish
- [ ] Giant Pacific octopus
- [ ] Common bottlenose dolphin

Tropical rain forest

CHECKLIST

Use the stickers in this book to fill this lush tropical scene. Here are some animals that live in the rain forest:

- [ ] Western gorilla
- [ ] Toco toucan
- [ ] Green tree python
- [ ] Plumed basilisk
- [ ] Golden mantella
- [ ] Black-capped squirrel monkey

Dromedary

Brown
long-eared bat

South African
galago

Black-capped
squirrel
monkey

Large hairy armadillo

Ring-tailed
lemur

Western
gorilla

Lion

Red fox

African
wild dog

Maned wolf

Tiger

Bobcat

Gray wolf

Hippopotamus

Domestic cat

White rhinoceros

Brown bear

Giant panda

Sloth bear

Polar bear

West Indian manatee

Asian elephant

Giraffe

Walrus

Narwhal

Sperm whale

Orca

Blue whale

New Zealand sea lion

Common bottlenose dolphin

Tasmanian devil

Common wombat

Toco toucan

Arctic tern

Virginia opossum

Barn owl

Red kangaroo

Great cormorant

Blue tit

Black swan

Lesser flamingo

European starling

Black-crowned night heron

Yellow warbler

Bullock's oriole

Mallard

Wandering albatross

Brown pelican

Bald eagle

Common kestrel

Atlantic puffin

Secretary bird

Red-tailed hawk

Brown kiwi

Common ostrich

Tuatara

King penguin

African helmeted turtle

Leatherback turtle

Green tree python

Southern cassowary

Gila monster

Plumed basilisk

Galápagos tortoise

Indian starred tortoise

Panther chameleon

Red spitting cobra

Red-eared slider

Slow worm

Yellow anaconda

Adder

Common garter snake

Gharial

Spectacled caiman

American alligator

Nile crocodile

Golden mantella

Red-eyed tree frog

Fire salamander

Oriental fire-bellied toad

Purple caecilian

Southern leopard frog

Cuyaba dwarf frog

Axolotl

Tiger salamander

Great crested newt

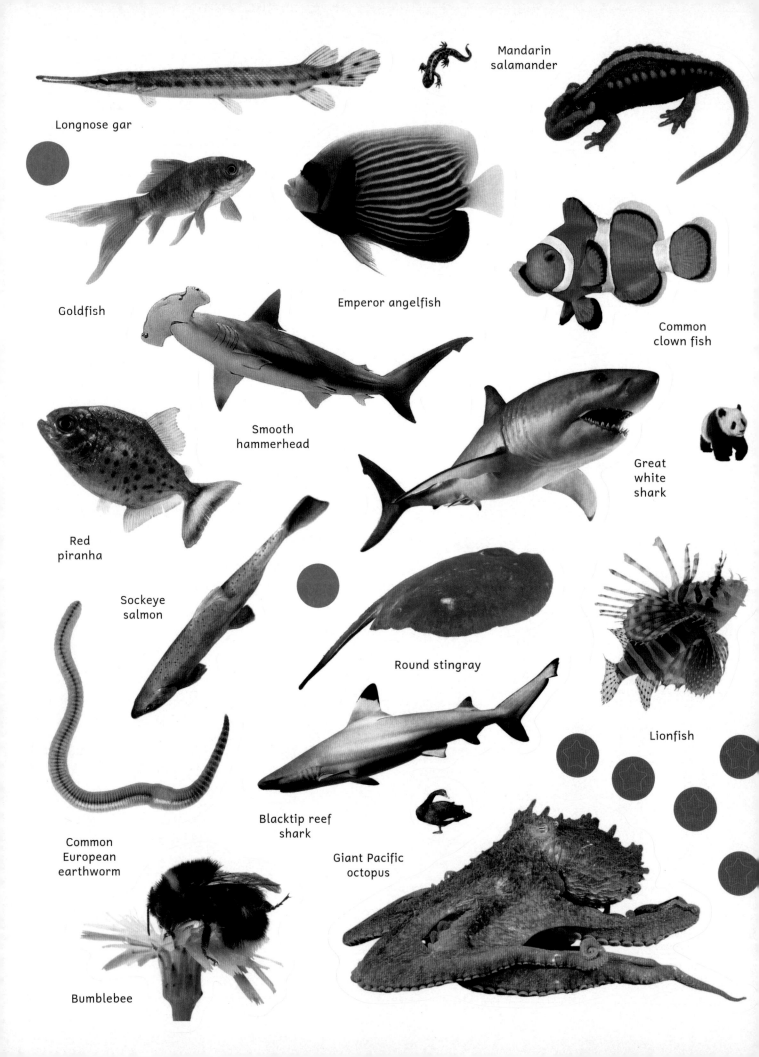

Longnose gar

Mandarin salamander

Goldfish

Emperor angelfish

Common clown fish

Smooth hammerhead

Great white shark

Red piranha

Sockeye salmon

Round stingray

Lionfish

Common European earthworm

Blacktip reef shark

Giant Pacific octopus

Bumblebee

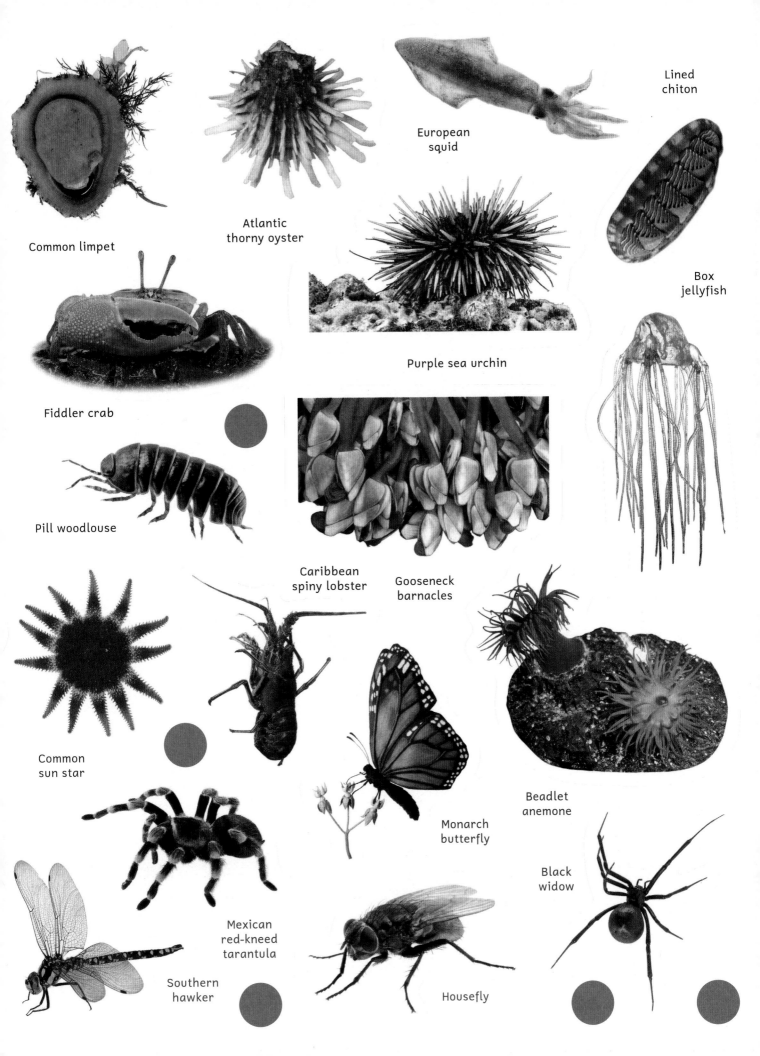

Common limpet

Atlantic
thorny oyster

European
squid

Lined
chiton

Box
jellyfish

Fiddler crab

Purple sea urchin

Pill woodlouse

Caribbean
spiny lobster

Gooseneck
barnacles

Common
sun star

Monarch
butterfly

Beadlet
anemone

Mexican
red-kneed
tarantula

Black
widow

Southern
hawker

Housefly

Jumping spider

Imperial scorpion

Golden scarab

Stickers for the grassland scene on pages 36-37

Tiger

Red-tailed hawk

Maned wolf

Red spitting cobra

Secretary bird

White rhinoceros

Giraffe

Stickers for the ocean scene on pages 38-39

European squid

Common sun star

Lionfish

Giant Pacific octopus

Arctic tern

Common
bottlenose dolphin

Orca

West Indian
manatee

Box jellyfish

Stickers for the rain forest scene on page 40

Golden mantella

Toco
toucan

Black-capped
squirrel monkey

Plumed
basilisk

Green tree
python

Western gorilla

Extra stickers